W9-AUF-652

13 Pop, Rock, Country and Dance Music Chartbusters

ARRANGED BY DAN COATES

Contents

Produced by
Alfred Music Publishing Co., Inc.
P.O. Box 10003
Van Nuys, CA 91410-0003
alfred.com

Printed in USA.

ISBN-10: 0-7390-6525-4
ISBN-13: 978-0-7390-6525-9

All Summer Long

Words and Music by
Matthew Shafer, R.J. Ritchie, Warren Zevon, Leroy Marinell,
Waddy Wachtel, Ed King, Gary Rossington and Ronnie Van Zant
Arranged by Dan Coates

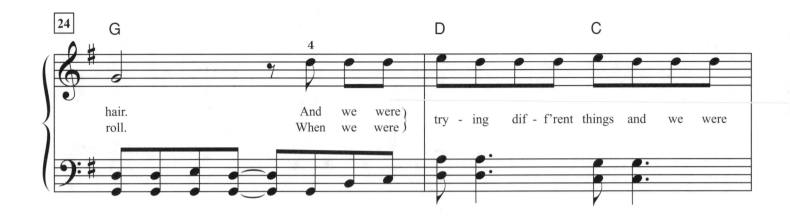

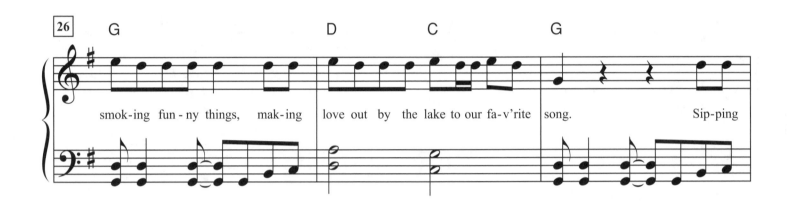

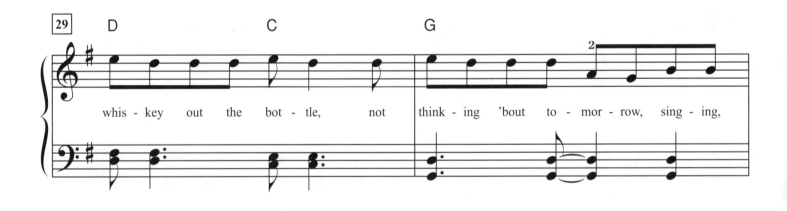

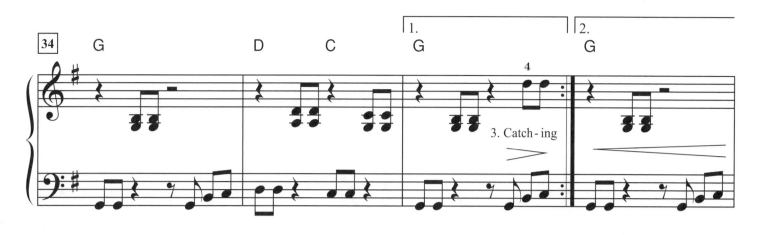

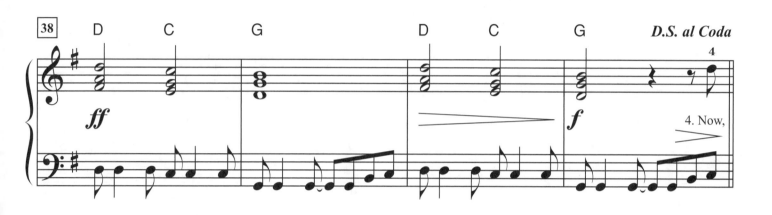

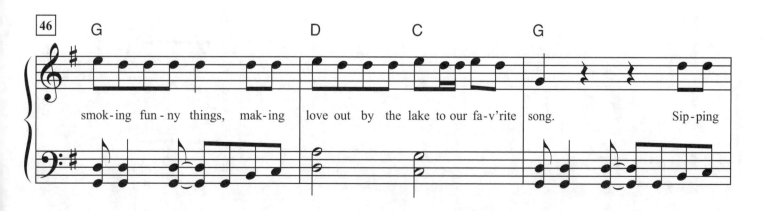

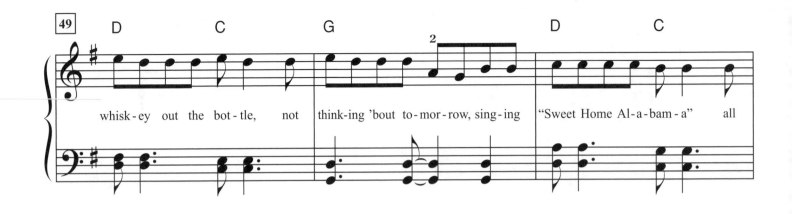

whisk-ey out the bot-tle, not think-ing 'bout to-mor-row, sing-ing "Sweet Home Al-a-bam-a" all

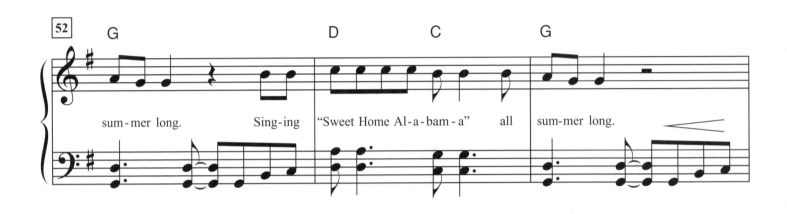

sum-mer long. Sing-ing "Sweet Home Al-a-bam-a" all sum-mer long.

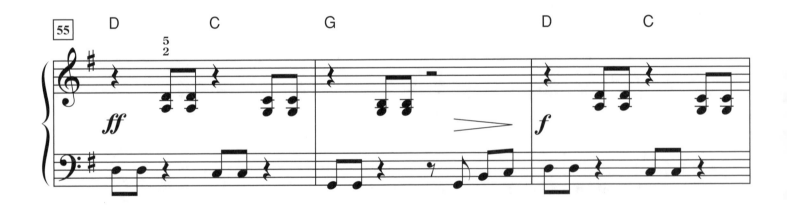

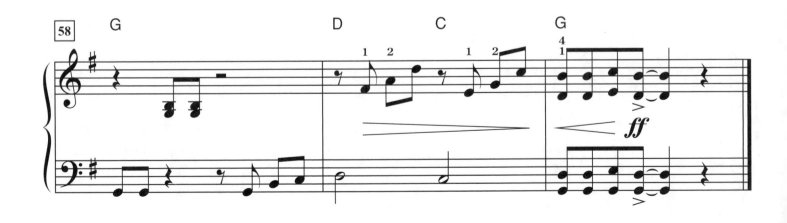

Decode

Words and Music by
Hayley Williams, Josh Farro and Taylor York
Arranged by Dan Coates

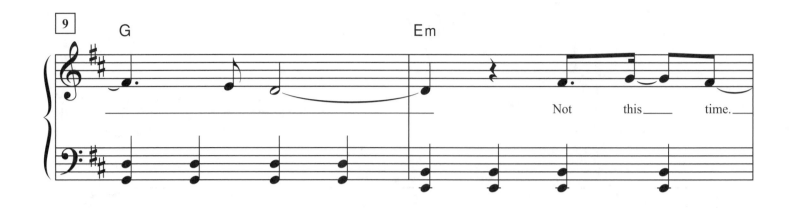

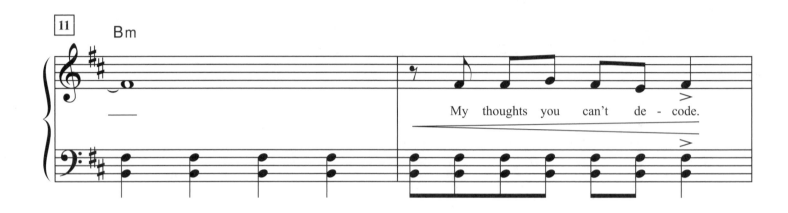

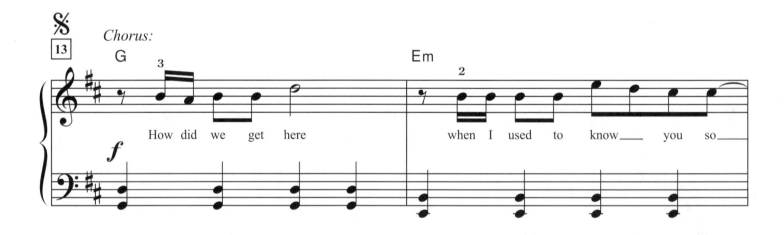

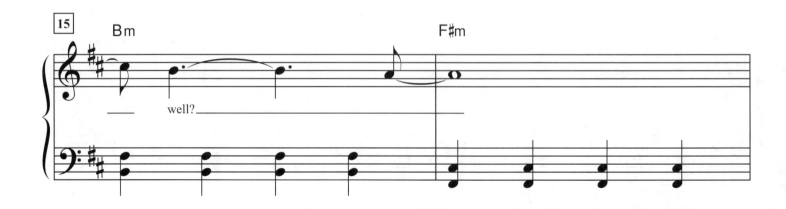

But how did we get here? Well, I think I know.

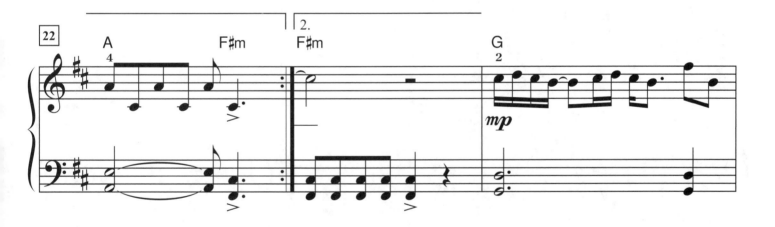

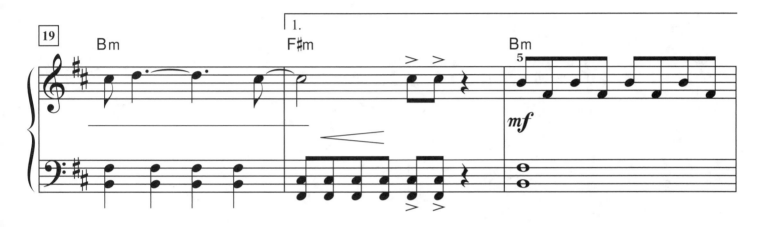

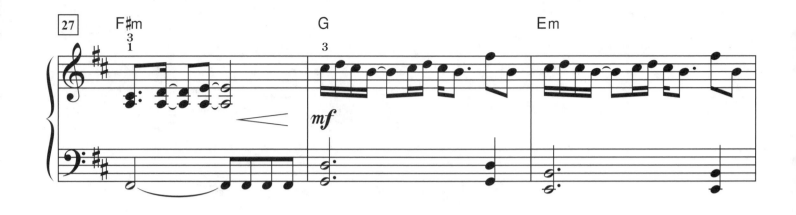

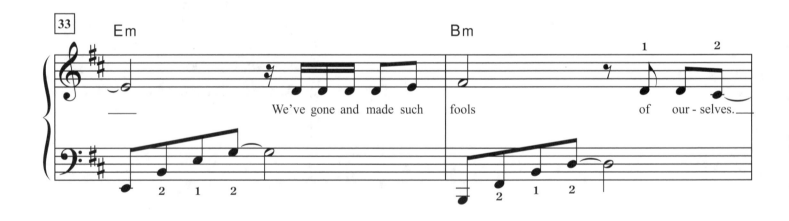

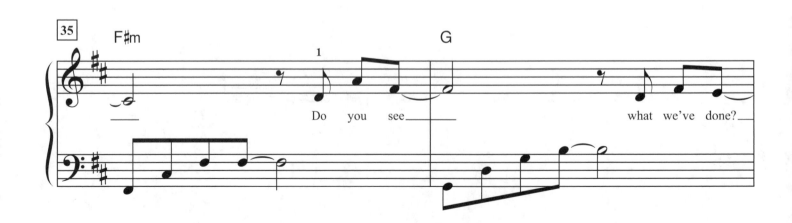

Verse 2:
The truth is hiding in your eyes
And it's hanging on your tongue.
Just boiling in my blood,
But you think that I can't see
What kind of man that you are,
If you're a man at all.
Well, I will figure this one out on my own.
On my own.
(To Chorus:)

Fame

Music by Michael Gore
Lyrics by Dean Pitchford
Arranged by Dan Coates

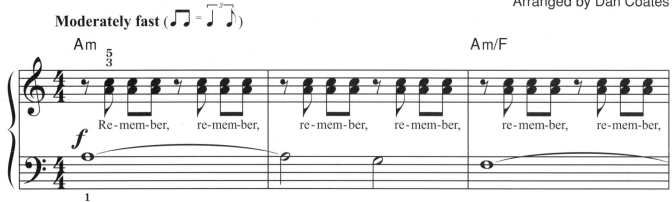

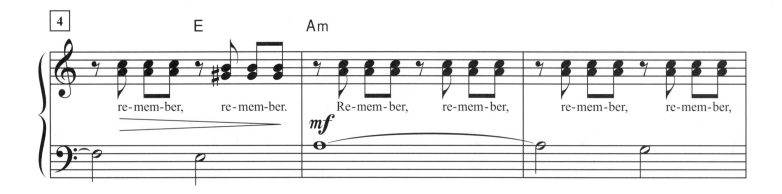

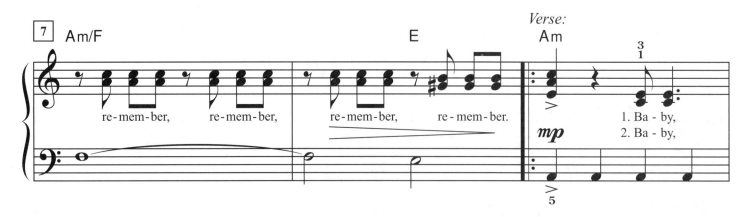

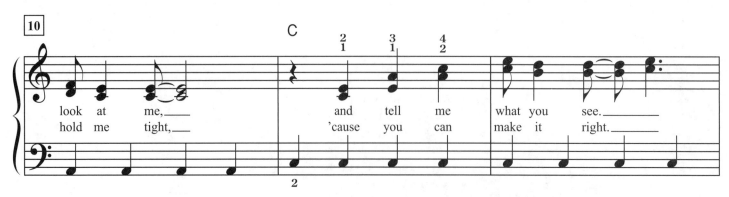

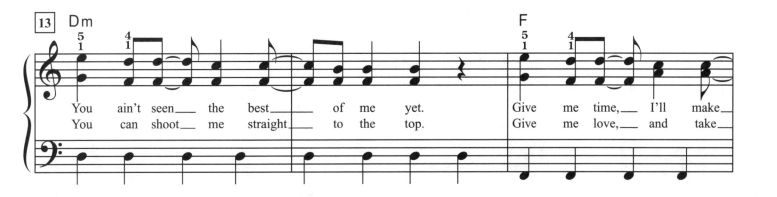
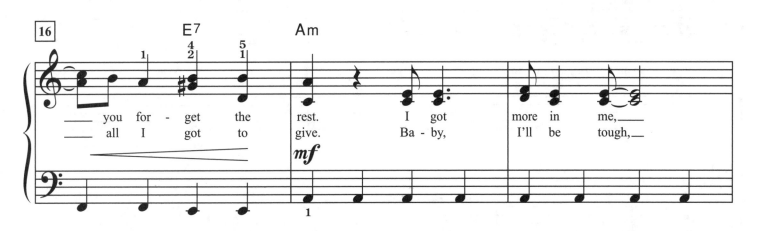

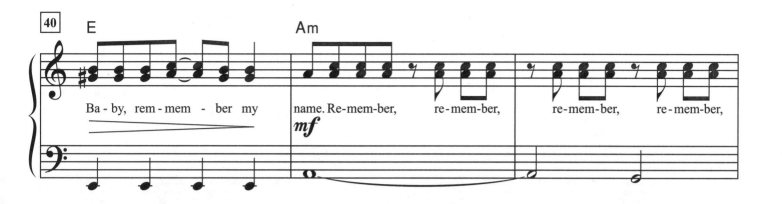

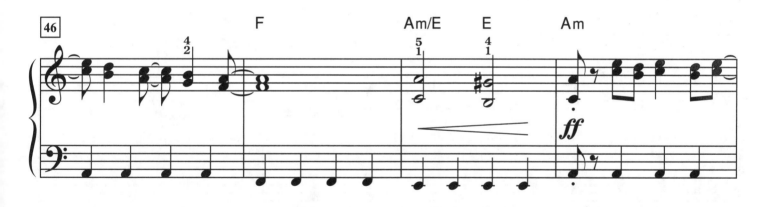

Home Sweet Home

Words and Music by
Nikki Sixx, Vince Neil and Tommy Lee
Arranged by Dan Coates

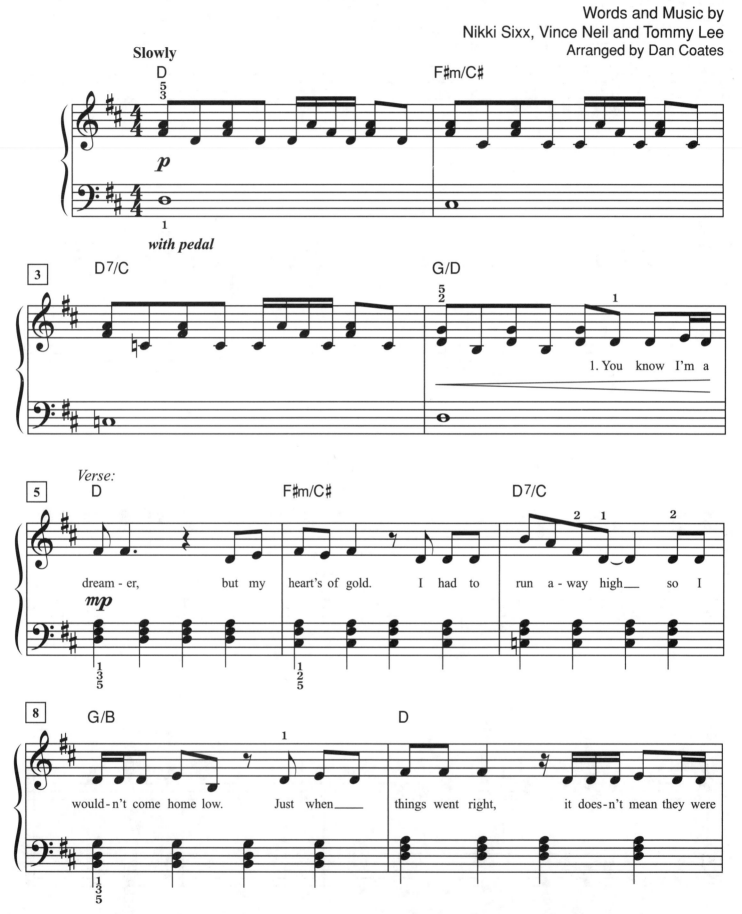

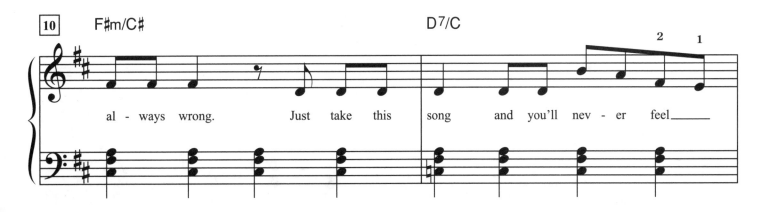

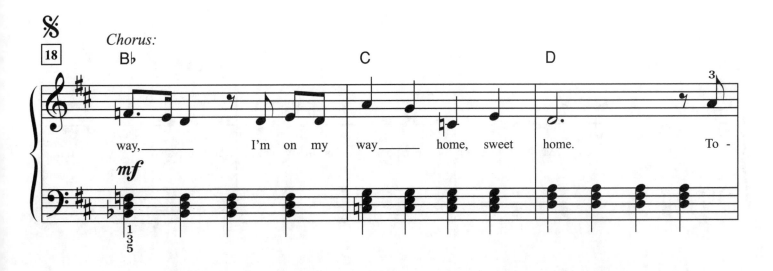

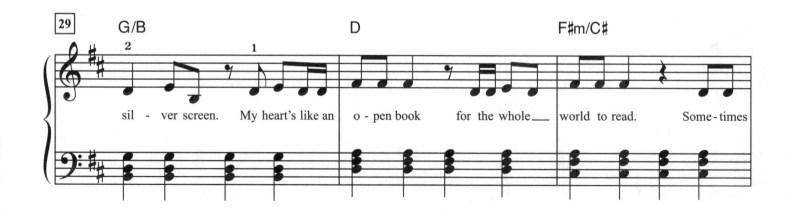

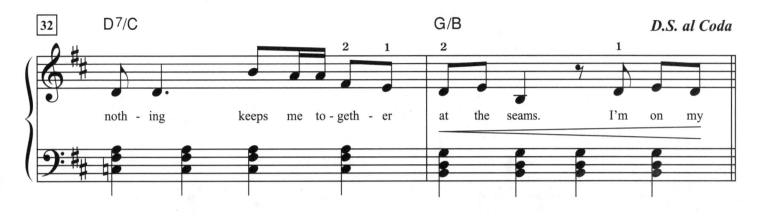

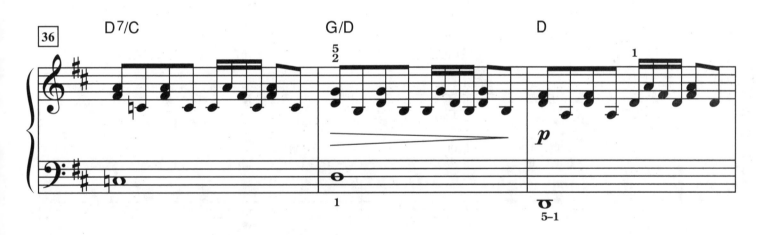

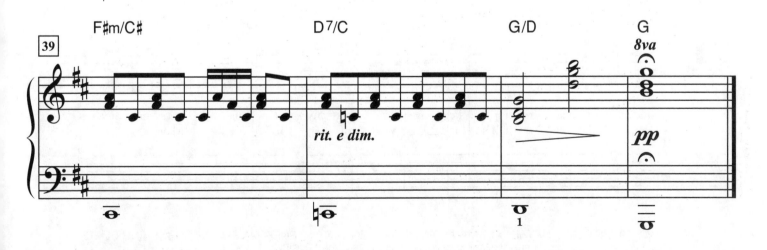

Haven't Met You Yet

Words and Music by
Michael Bublé, Alan Chang and Amy Foster
Arranged by Dan Coates

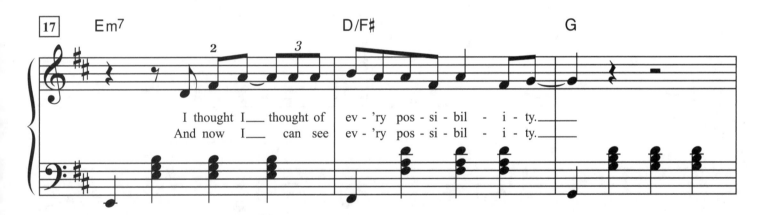

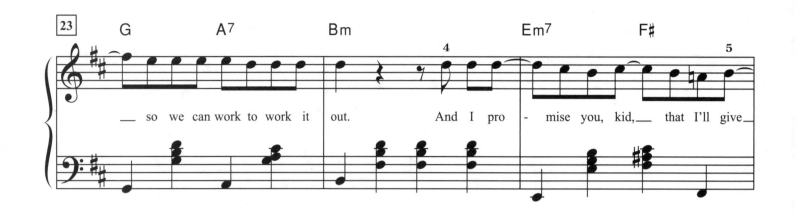

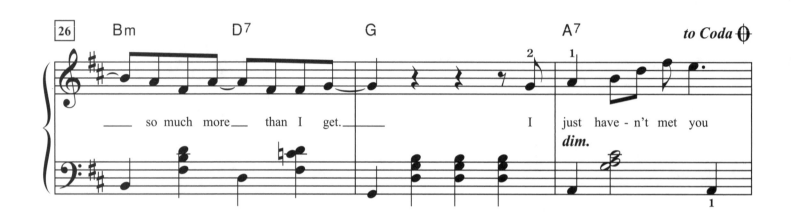

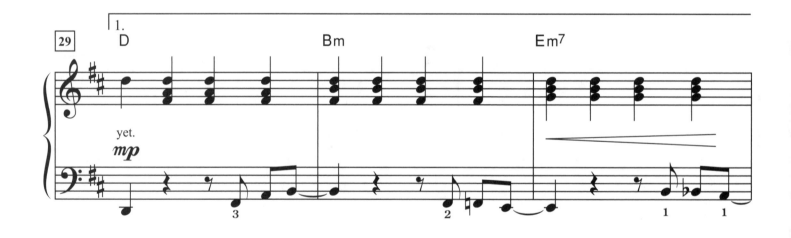

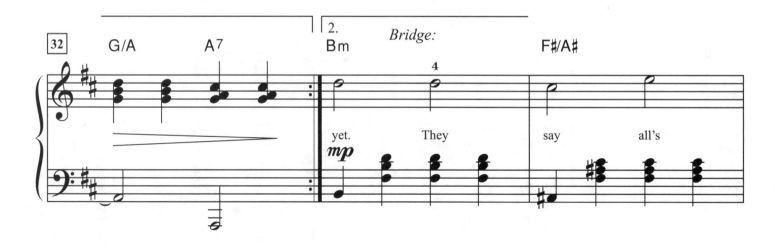

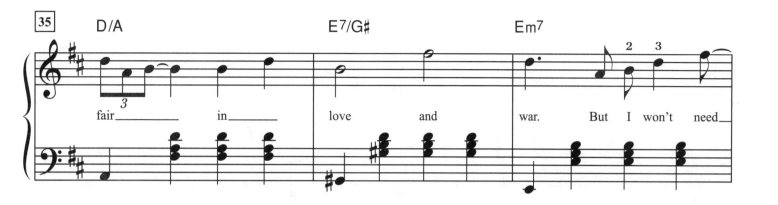

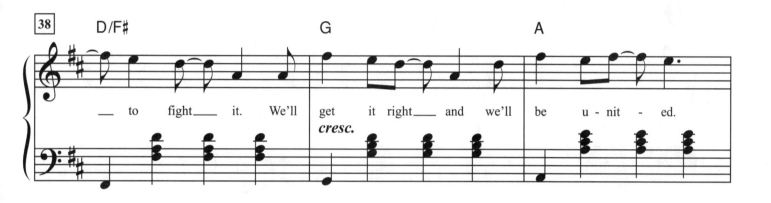

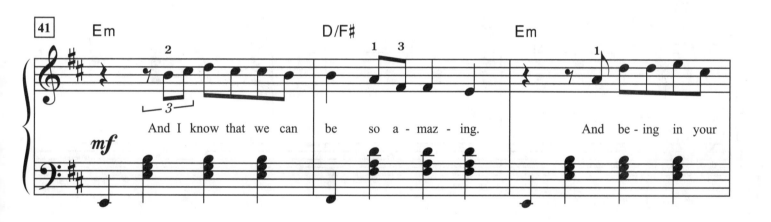

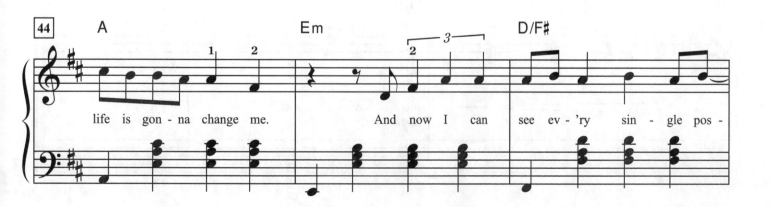

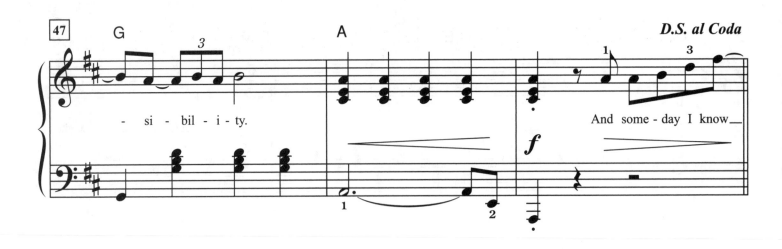

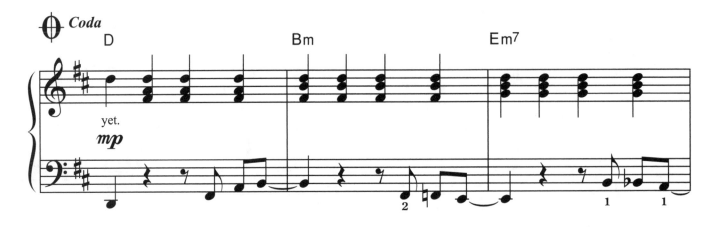

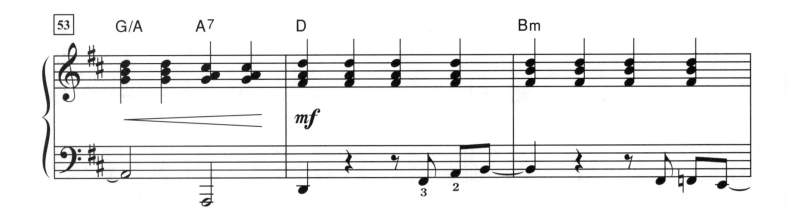

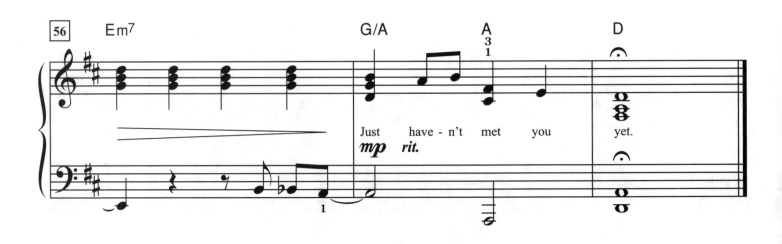

I Didn't Know My Own Strength

Words and Music by Diane Warren
Arranged by Dan Coates

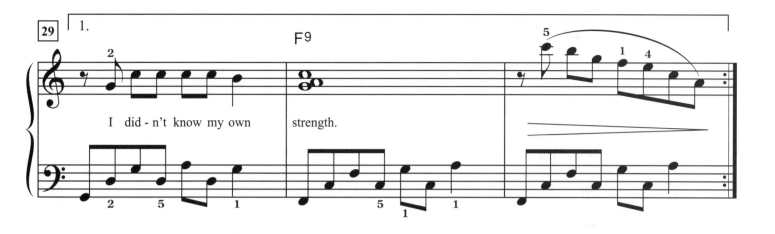

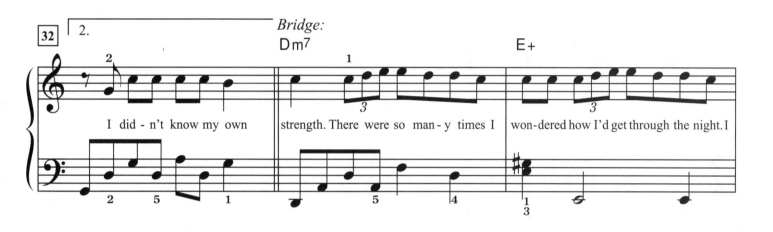

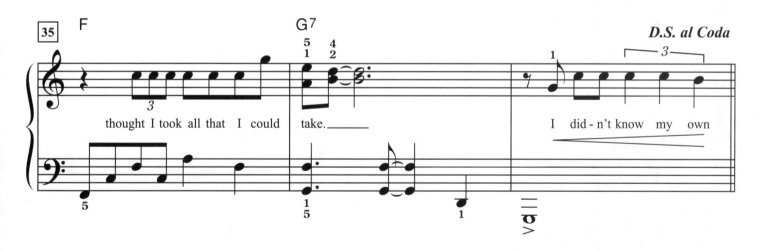

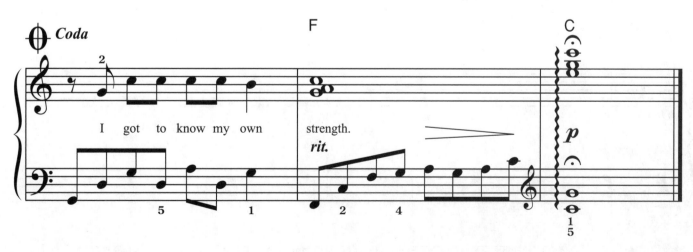

If Today Was Your Last Day

Words and Music by Chad Kroeger
Arranged by Dan Coates

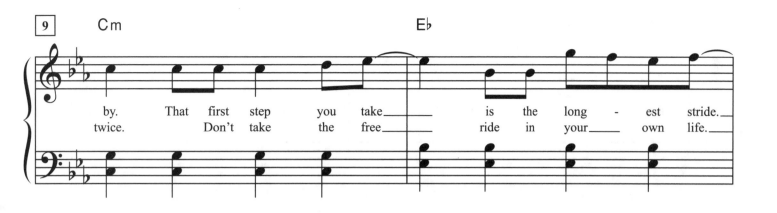

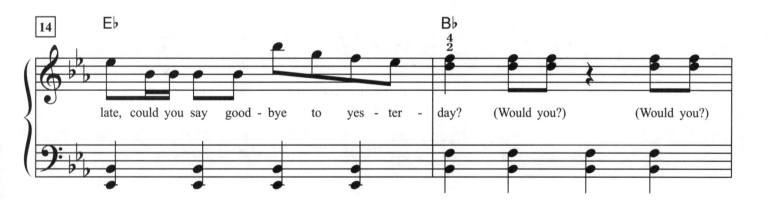

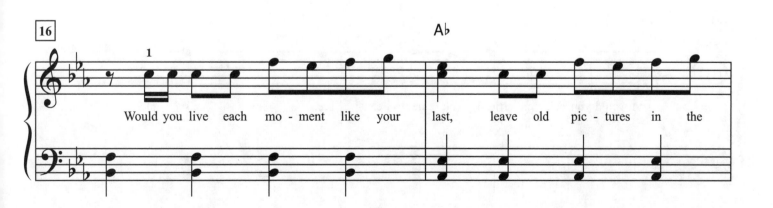

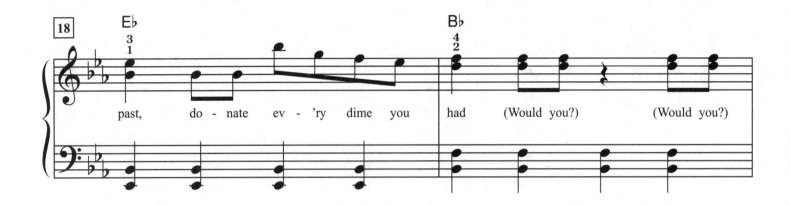

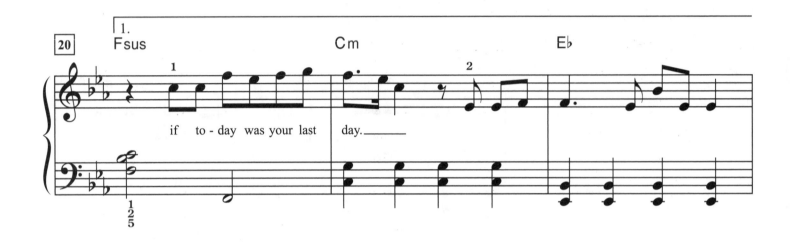

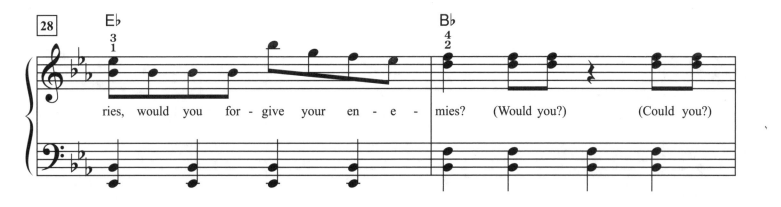

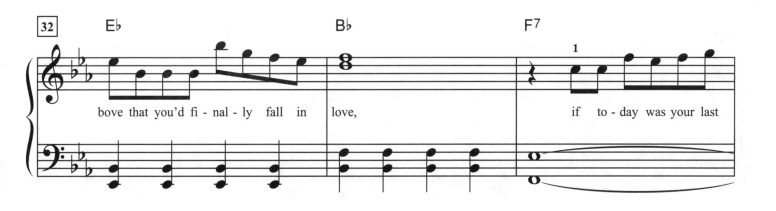

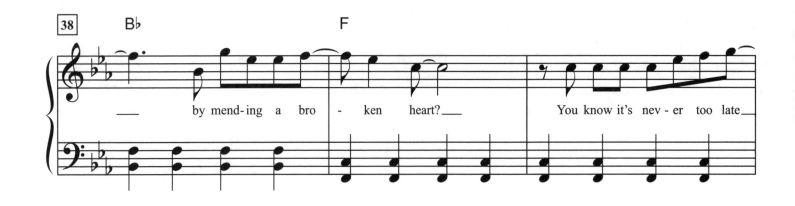

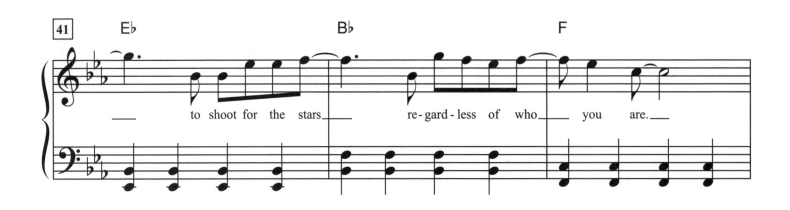

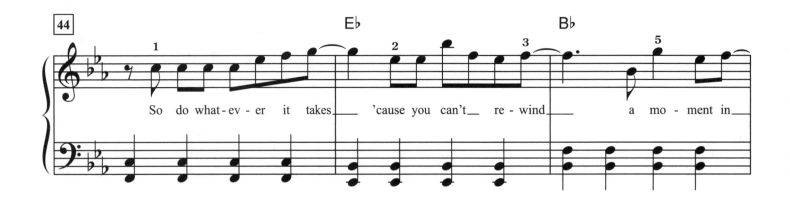

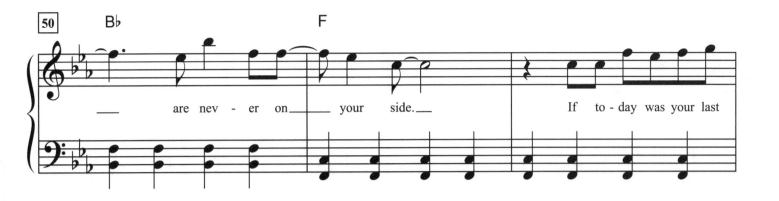

are nev - er on ___ your side. ___ If to - day was your last

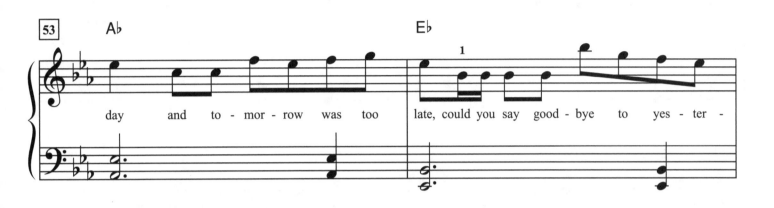

day and to - mor - row was too late, could you say good - bye to yes - ter -

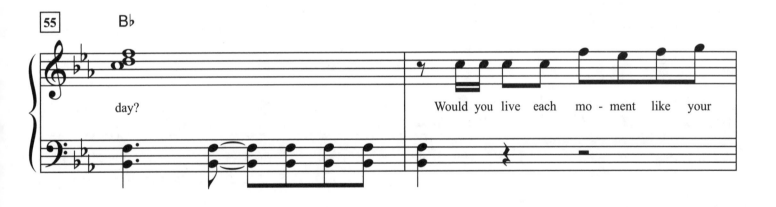

day? Would you live each mo - ment like your

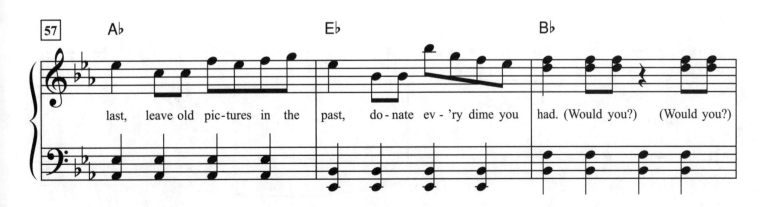

last, leave old pic - tures in the past, do - nate ev - 'ry dime you had. (Would you?) (Would you?)

Know Your Enemy

Lyrics by Billie Joe
Music by Green Day
Arranged by Dan Coates

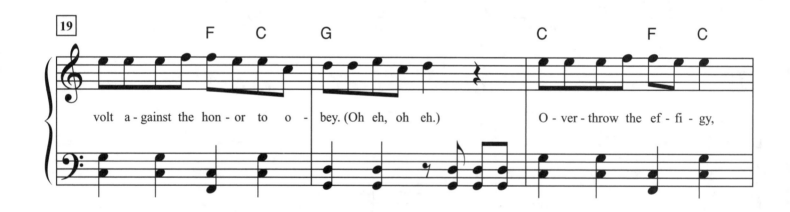

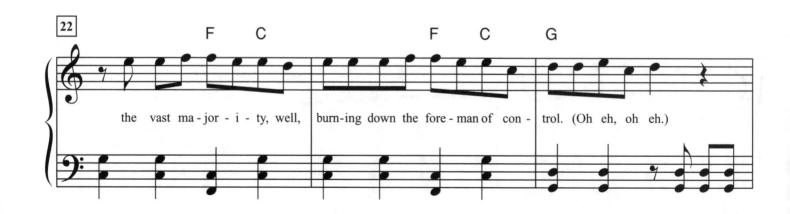

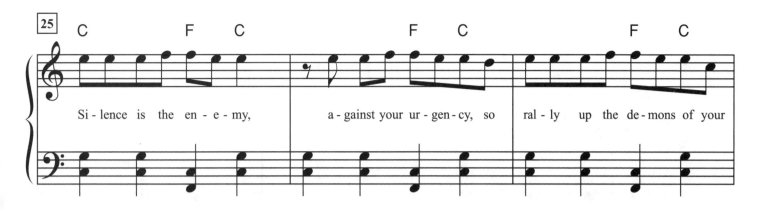

25 C   F   C   F   C   F   C

Si - lence is the en - e - my,   a - gainst your ur - gen - cy, so   ral - ly up the de - mons of your

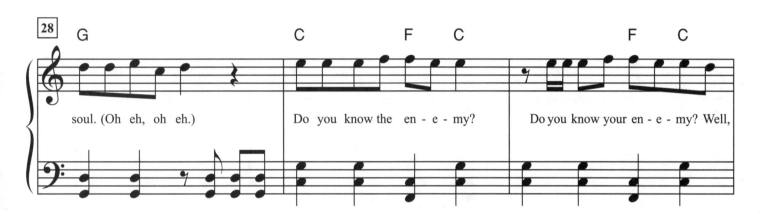

28 G   C   F   C   F   C

soul. (Oh eh, oh eh.)   Do you know the en - e - my?   Do you know your en - e - my? Well,

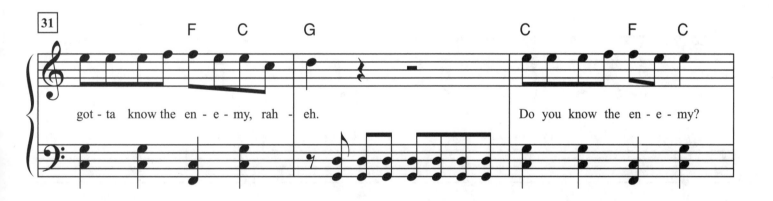

31   F   C   G   C   F   C

got - ta know the en - e - my, rah -   eh.   Do you know the en - e - my?

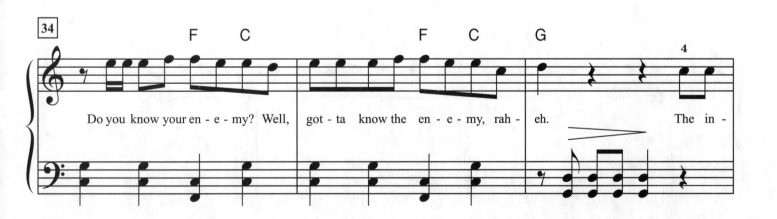

34   F   C   F   C   G   4

Do you know your en - e - my? Well,   got - ta know the en - e - my, rah -   eh.   The in -

38

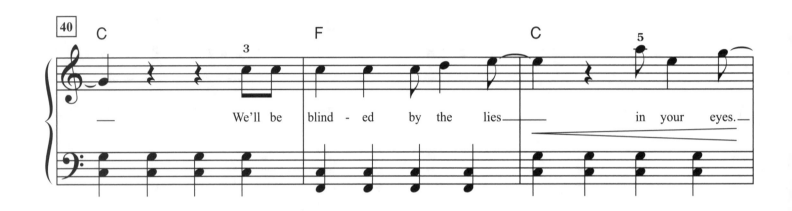

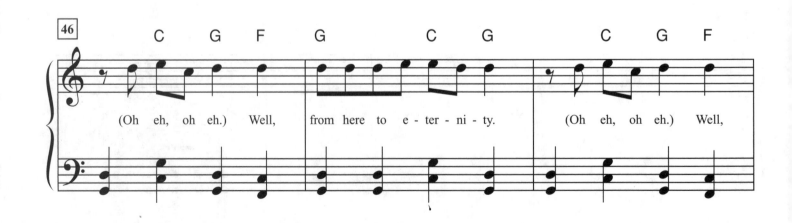

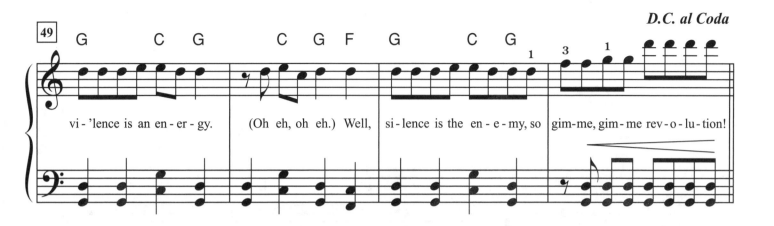

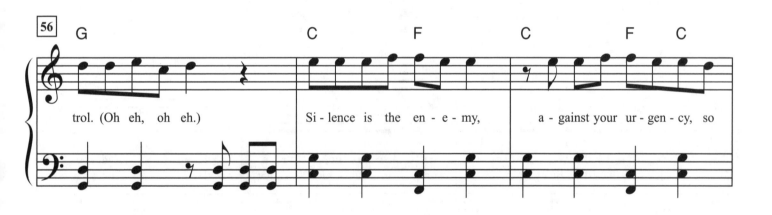

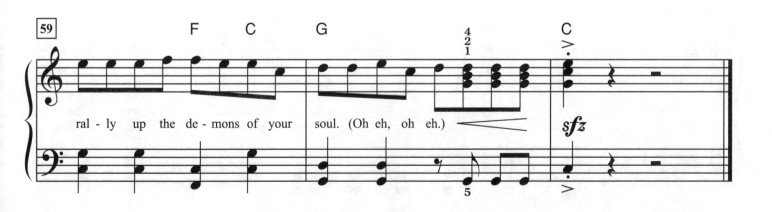

Let It Rock

Words and Music by
Kevin Rudolf and Dwayne Carter
Arranged by Dan Coates

Steady rock beat

Verse:

F G D

1. I see your dir - ty face, high be - hind your col - lar. What is

son's dis - graced, he who knew his fa - ther. When he

F G D Bb G

done in vain, truth is hard to swal - low. So you pray to God, to jus -

cursed his name, turned and chased the dol - lar, but it broke his heart, so he

D Bb G D

- ti - fy the way you live a lie, live a lie, live a lie. And you take

stuck his mid - dle fin - ger to the world, to the world, to the world. And you take

F G D F G

your time, and you do your crime.

your time, and you stand in line

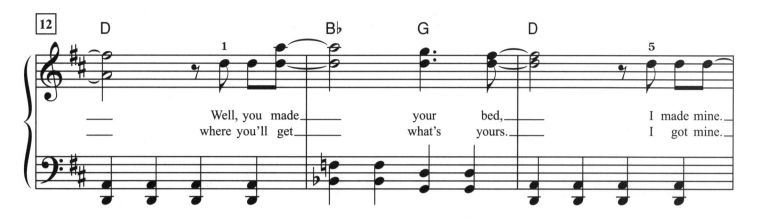

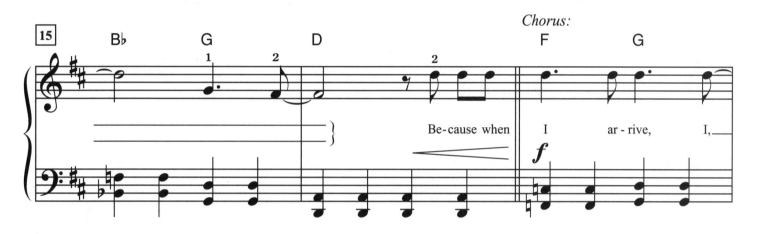

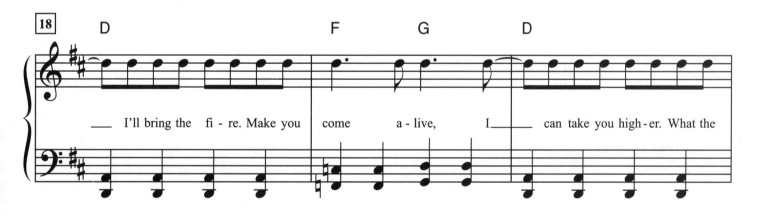

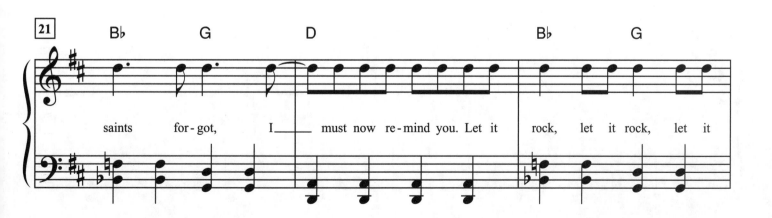

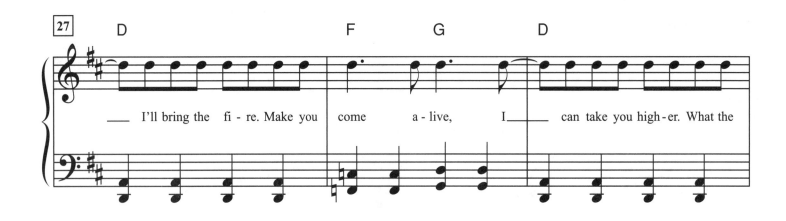

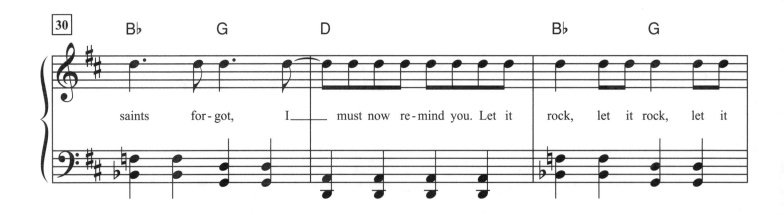

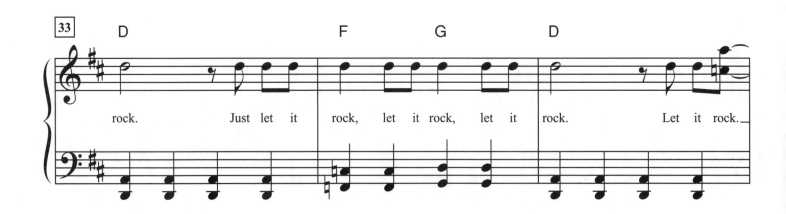

My Life Would Suck Without You

Words and Music by
Claude Kelly, Lukasz Gottwald and Max Martin
Arranged by Dan Coates

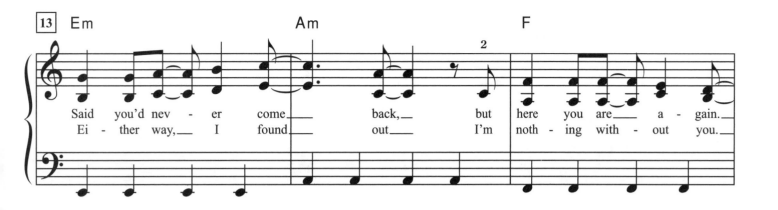

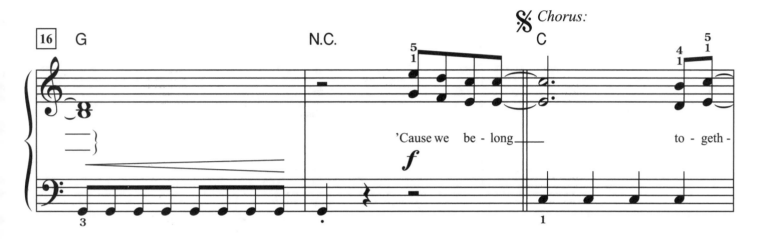

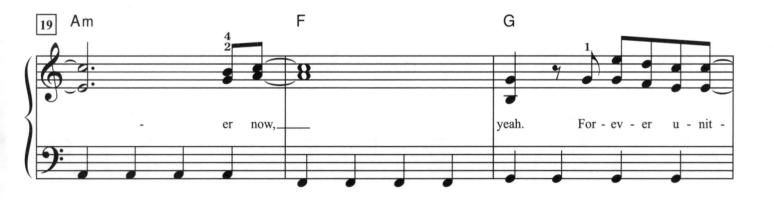

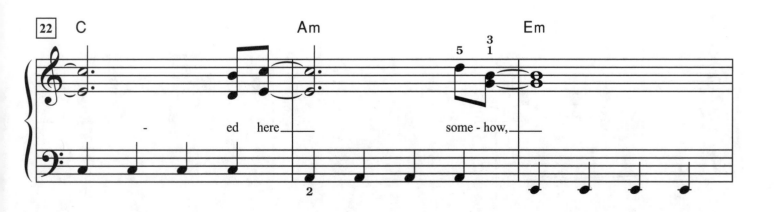

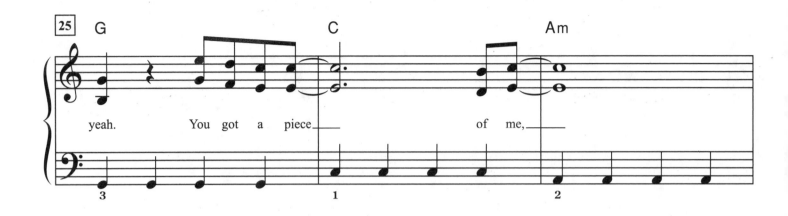

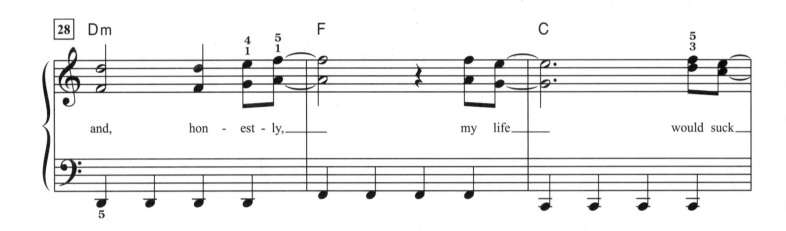

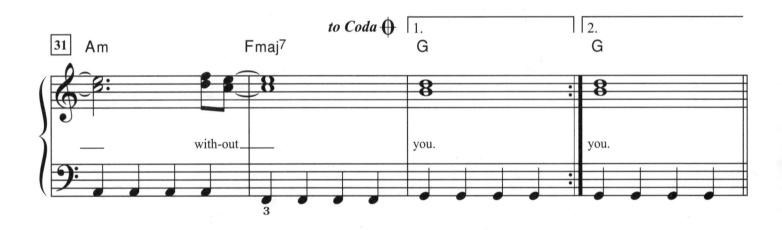

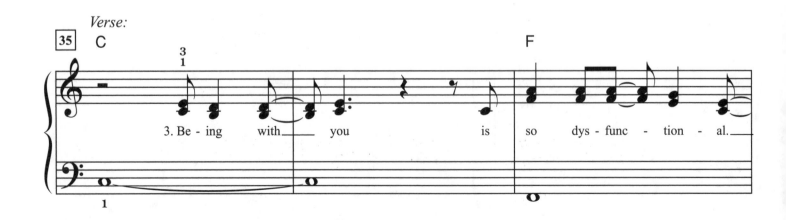

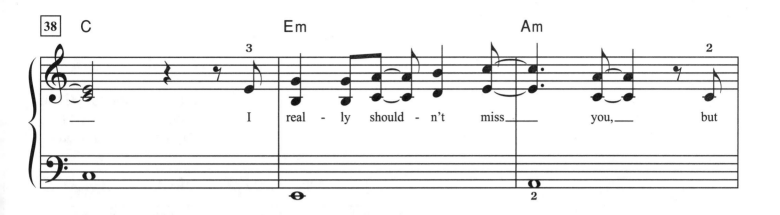

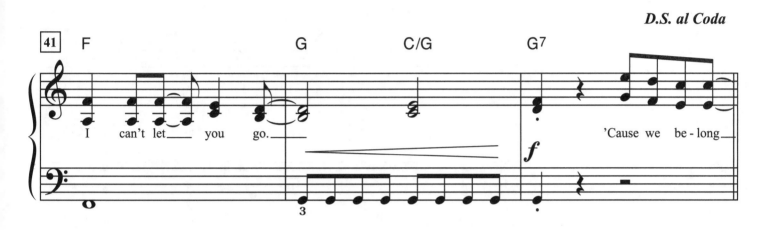

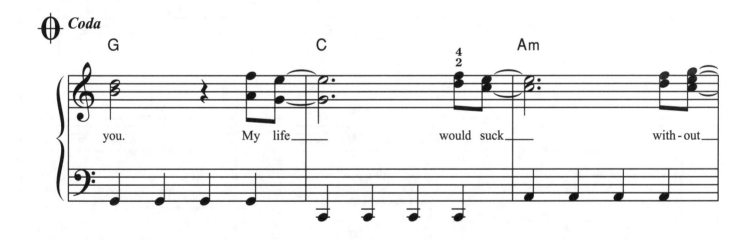

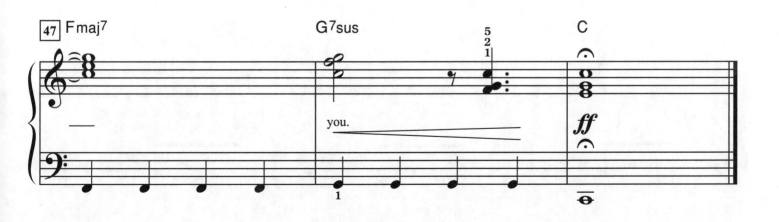

Out Here on My Own

Music by Michael Gore
Lyrics by Lesley Gore
Arranged by Dan Coates

49

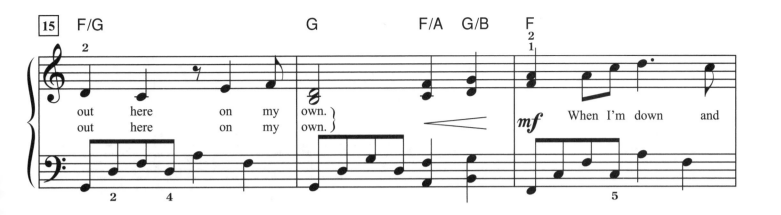

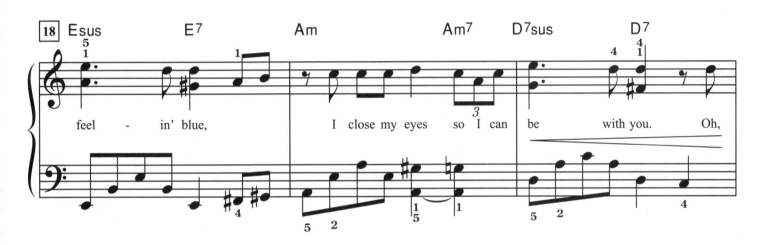

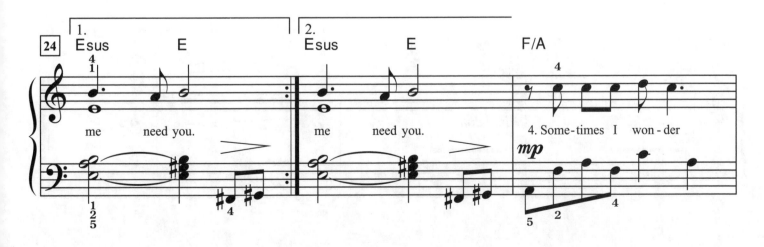

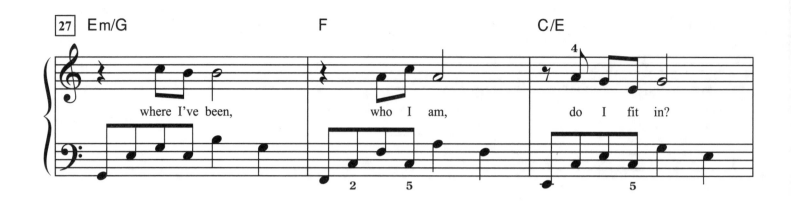

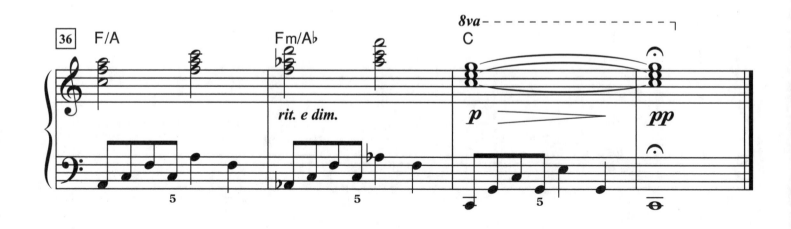

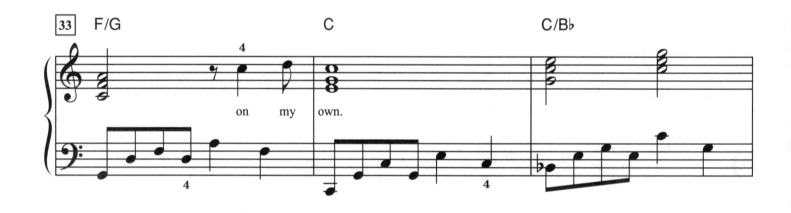

Shuttin' Detroit Down

Words and Music by
John Rich and John D. Anderson
Arranged by Dan Coates

52

go your way._____   Now

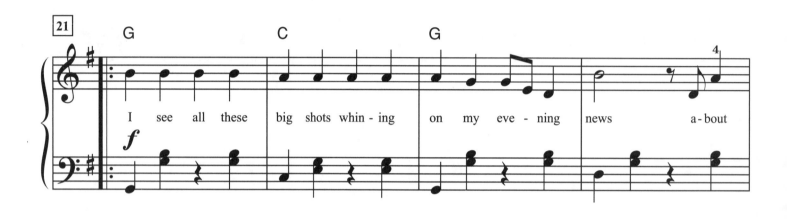

I see all these big shots whin - ing on my eve - ning news a - bout

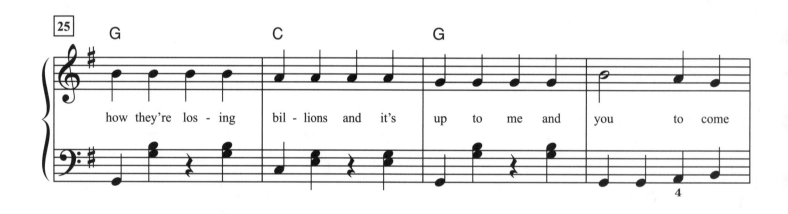

how they're los - ing bil - lions and it's up to me and you to come

run - ning___ to___   the

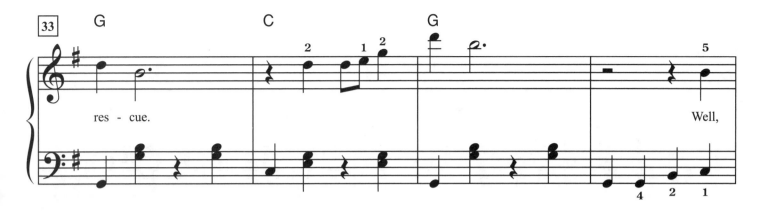

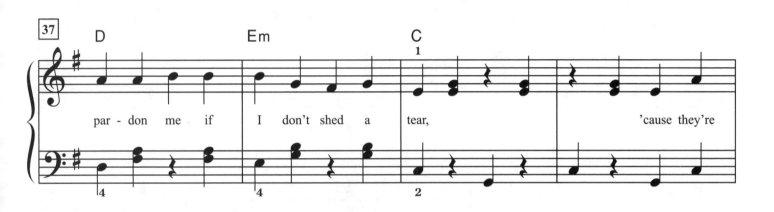

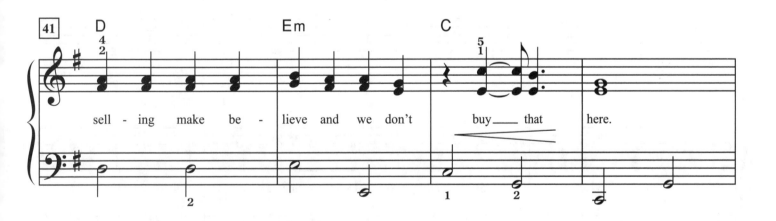

Chorus:

55

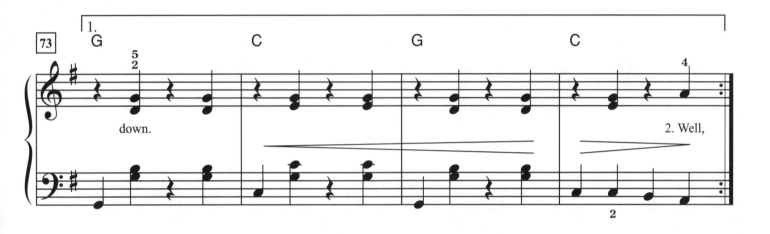

(Verse 2:)
Well, that old man's been working
In that plant most all his life.
Now his pension plan's been cut in half
And he can't afford to die.
And it's a crying shame
'Cause he ain't the one to blame.
When I looked down and see his calloused hands
Well, let me tell you, friend
It gets me fighting mad.
(To Chorus:)

Waking Up in Vegas

Words and Music by
Katy Perry, Andreas Carlsson and Desmond Child
Arranged by Dan Coates

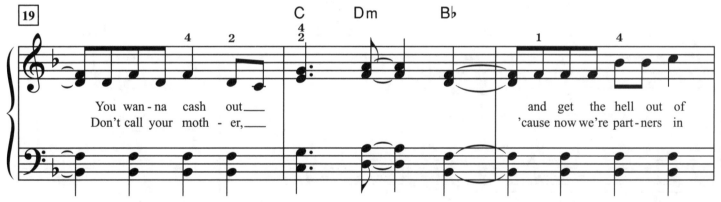

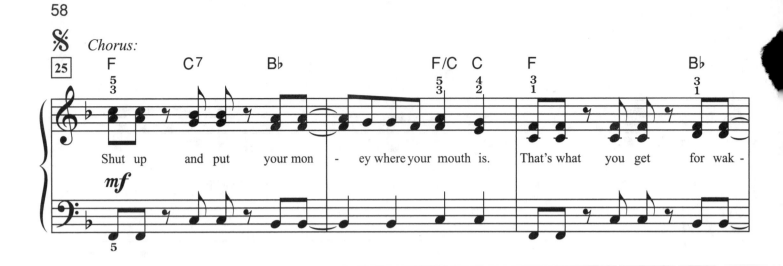

Chorus:

Shut up and put your mon - ey where your mouth is. That's what you get for wak-

- ing up in Ve - gas. Get up and shake the glit - ter off your clothes, now.

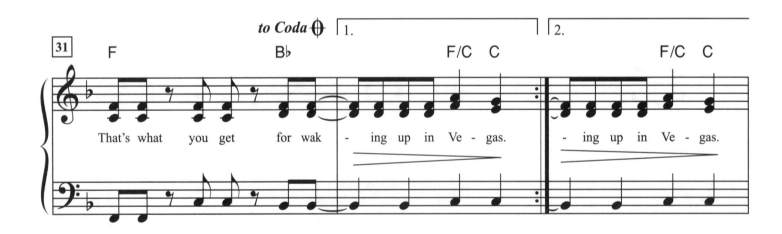

to Coda ⊕ 1. 2.

That's what you get for wak - ing up in Ve - gas. - ing up in Ve - gas.

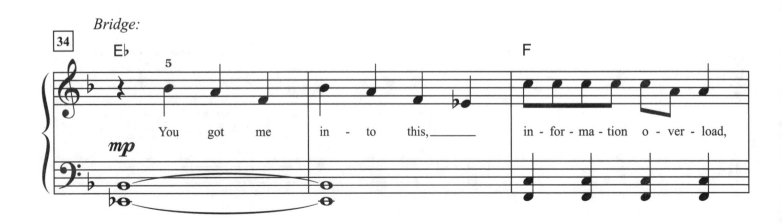

Bridge:

You got me in - to this,_____ in - for - ma - tion o - ver - load,